BRAIN-BALANCE
BOOSTER

50 puzzles to improve your thinking

CHARLES PHILLIPS

CONNECTIONS
BOOK PUBLISHING

For JDP

A CONNECTIONS EDITION
This edition published in Great Britain in 2014 by
Connections Book Publishing Limited
St Chad's House, 148 King's Cross Road, London WC1X 9DH
www.connections-publishing.com

Text and puzzles copyright © Bibelot Limited 2014
This edition copyright © Eddison Sadd Editions 2014

The right of Charles Phillips to be identified as the author of the work
has been asserted by him in accordance with the Copyright,
Designs and Patents Act 1988.

British Library Cataloguing-in-Publication data available on request.

ISBN 978-1-85906-385-9

1   3   5   7   9   10   8   6   4   2

Phototypeset in Cafeteria and Vectora LH using InDesign on Apple Macintosh
Printed in Hong Kong

BRAIN-BALANCE
BOOSTER

CONTENTS

Introduction

Do you enjoy speaking, coming up with words, and maintaining a conversational flow? Or do you prefer losing yourself in a book, being immersed in the world of the story, seeing and feeling its colors and sensations?

If you're dealing with a sequence of words, are you good at predicting what will come next? Or are you better at remembering the details of what has gone before?

Our intriguing—and sometimes rather mysterious—thinking preferences and differing strengths in mental performance arise from the brain's split into left and right.

The upper part of the brain is divided into two hemispheres, and particular types of mental processing are stronger in each half: the left brain is especially involved in producing language, while the right brain plays a key role in generating the feelings and sensations that come with reading the words of a novel.

In math, your left brain is engaged in counting or recalling your times tables; the right, in estimating quantities. When you're using or hearing language, left-brain activity supports predicting combinations of words, while the right brain is engaged in remembering details in a sequence. You rely more on your left brain when understanding the literal meaning of the words, and depend on your right brain to glean meaning from emphasis and intonation.

Are you a left or right brainer? Experimental research in the 1960s indicated that the brain's left and right sides were semi-independent, showing more or less activity when undertaking particular mental tasks. For example, the left was more active when doing math problems; the right, when comparing colors.

From this grew the popular distinction between left-brain and right-brain people. According to this, left-brain thinkers were good at thinking logically and rationally and doing mathematics (logicians and scientists), while right-brain thinkers were more creative and intuitive, better at visual tasks (artists and creatives).

Today's neuroscientists caution against dividing people in this way. Thinking involves the whole brain. Certain brain regions combine dynamically in networks according to the task at hand. But the brain's two halves do have specialisms—they do perform particular types of processing. They draw separate meanings from incoming material, perceive reality differently. Occasionally they are liable to make contrasting choices. This system developed to boost efficiency. Tasks are divided and the brain's two halves process things semi-independently.

Declining difference The disparities in processing between left and right brain tend to reduce as we grow older. Scientists are not sure why. Perhaps the brain becomes less good at dividing tasks between the hemispheres and combining the responses? Or it may be that older people bring both halves of the brain to bear in order to compensate for the natural decline in functioning. Either way, studying variations in processing between left- and right-brain hemispheres seems to offer a fruitful way of investigating means of limiting natural decline in brain performance.

Potential to change Although it no longer makes sense to divide people into left-brain or right-brain thinkers, it remains true to say that we can be stronger in either left-brain processing or right-brain processing.

And we should never view these differences as defining us. The brain is changing right through life, making new combinations

7

among its millions of brain cells as we learn new things and try out fresh approaches. In fact, your brain makes 1 million new connections among its neurons every single second.

The truth is, we can all benefit from being aware of our strengths and working at our weaker areas. We each have tremendous potential to change. One key thing: Aim for balance. Let's face it, these are challenging times—and we need to bring all our resources to bear in our thinking. Try to enliven logical analysis with intuitive leaps. Enrich dry material with color and visual flair. Switch from the detail to the big picture and back again.

The left-brain/right-brain distinction is a neat way to characterize our varying responses, strengths, and weaknesses—and it provides a very useful frame for our efforts to balance our thinking.

How the book works First, try Thinking Challenge 1 (pages 11–14), designed to test your thinking style in a real-life scenario, then check pages 92–3 to see how you fared. Next, answer the Left-Brain/Right-Brain Questionnaire (page 15) to learn how your thinking is currently balanced. Work out your total Starting Score (see page 93), then begin with Left or Right Puzzle 1.

The cross-wired brain and our sense of time

Your brain is cross-wired so that the left hemisphere controls the right side of the body and the right hemisphere commands the body's left side. Stroke damage to one side of the brain can result in paralysis on the body's opposite side. Remarkably, this can affect our perception of time. Western people typically understand time to be flowing from left (the past) to right (the future). Research at the University of Geneva showed that people with damage to the right side of the brain had trouble thinking of the past (the left). In a test, they assigned past events to the future.

Proceed now through the fifty puzzles, which are intended to develop your skills in typically left-brain processes, such as logical thought, and typically right-brain processes, for instance, spatial perception. Difficulty levels range from 1 to 5, so you can be sure your brain will be stretched to the limit. After each puzzle, to find out where to go next, score yourself between 0 and 5, depending on whether you got the answer right and how easy you found it (from 0 for very hard and incorrect, to 5 for very easy and correct).

- Scores of 0, 1, or 2 lead to a puzzle of the same kind.
- Scores of 3, 4, or 5 lead to a puzzle of the other kind.

For example, if you start with Left Puzzle 1 and score 3, 4, or 5, indicating a degree of success, proceed to Right Puzzle 1. But if you score 0, 1, or 2, indicating that you struggled with it to some extent, proceed to Left Puzzle 2. You always proceed to the next question in the numerical L or R sequence. So, you might proceed like this: L1–L2–L3–R1–L4–R2–R3–R4–L5. Or like this: R1–R2–R3–R4–R5–L1–R6–L2–L3. (You don't need to total up your scores as you work through the book—they're only there to tell you where to go next—but do mark them so you can judge your performance at the end. See page 94 for guidance.)

The aim is to attempt all fifty puzzles, so if you do all the Left puzzles using the process described above, proceed through the remaining Right puzzles in numerical order; likewise, if you complete all the Right puzzles, proceed through the remaining Left puzzles in numerical order. Finally, take the climactic **Thinking Challenge 2** (pages 69–73) to gauge your progress overall.

Once you've worked your way through the book, you'll be well on your way to fine-tuning your brain and learning how to think *better*. You have a whole brain—now use it!

THINKING CHALLENGE 1

On the following pages you have the chance to evaluate the balance of typically right-brain and left-brain approaches in your thinking. Perhaps you rely on logic and analysis, or maybe you're a more intuitive thinker? Are you good at seeing how things fit together or does your strength lie more in predicting what will come next in a sequence? Are you confident in juggling numbers and calculating effectively on your feet? Work through the thinking challenge—"The Trouble I've Seen"—on pages 12–14 and then respond to the short questionnaire on page 15.

The challenge puts left-brain/right-brain differences and choices in a light-hearted, real-life context and is followed by questions that draw out the character of your typical behavior and thinking processes in a variety of everyday situations. Do your best to answer honestly; try to identify how you actually behave and think—rather than how you wish you could be.

Afterward, turn to pages 92–3 for guidance on scoring and assessing your response. Enjoy the challenge—and good luck!

"The Trouble I've Seen"

You're feeling seasick, but you're not actually at sea. You're an intern at an elite tour company. Despite your lowly status, you've had to jump on a riverboat to take over from your boss, who's not turned up, and you're having to lead a group tour. You look queasily at the company logo and tagline—"Maharaja: Elite travel services fit for the 1 percent."

You have a group of seven clients to care for. You look down at the file in your hand—a sheet of names and descriptions:

- **Jonty Gerrard:** blond, chubby, male, clean-shaven. Age 59. Venture capitalist. South African. Traveling alone. Recovering alcoholic.
- **Rebecca Mirviss:** pale skin, dark ponytail, brown eyes. Age 33. Fine art professor. American. Traveling with boyfriend Carter. Teetotal.
- **Nisha Cohen:** brown skin, black hair. Age 21. Jazz/blues vocalist. Asian-American. Married to Marco. Vegetarian.

Notes

- **Sir Charles Tattershall:** gray hair, beard. Age 65. Actor. English. Homes in London and Edinburgh. Traveling with civil partner Andrew.
- **Andrew Burns:** thick red hair, mustache. Age 56. Former policeman. Scottish.
- **Marco Cohen:** bald, clean-shaven, green eyes. Age 42. Jazz trumpeter. Canadian. Home in Montreal. Traveling with wife Nisha. Lactose intolerant.
- **Carter Phillips:** tall and very thin black man, Afro hair, brown eyes. Age 27. Designer and builder of bicycles. Barbadian. Home in NYC. Vegan.

A bald man and a blond man come up to you. Can you place their names without checking the list? They each have 15,000 US dollars to change into euros. Should you use the SmartCash bureau, which offers €0.65 to $1 with no fee, the bank department in Harrington department store, which offers €0.70/$1 with a 5 percent fee, or the traditional bank of the wealthy, Wodehouse and Williams, which offers €0.75/$1 with a 10 percent fee?

Notes

Problems keep piling up. You're a big fan of Louis Armstrong and just as you find yourself humming "Nobody Knows the Trouble I've Seen …" your phone rings and you're asked to memorize room numbers and order flowers and drinks for the guests at the Eden Hotel: Rebecca and Carter in the Adam and Eve Room (basement room 7), Sir Charles and Andrew in the Garden Rooms (first floor 2 and 3), Nisha and Marco in the Treetop Penthouse (9), and Jonty in the rooftop Sky Pavilion (5). How do you fare?

The boat docks, and the travelers are driven off in the limousines for the one-mile journey to the Eden. Your final task is to deal with the transfer of their baggage, after which there is a seat reserved for you in a normal cab. Each of your passengers has three bags of varying sizes. The guidance notes say that the Maharaja agency minivan has room for eighteen normal cases. What do you do?

(Turn to pages 92–3 for guidance on scoring and to find out how to assess your responses on this and the questions opposite.)

Notes

Left-Brain/Right-Brain Questionnaire

Tick the answers that ring true, then turn to page 93 to find out your Starting Score.

AGREE

1. On a lazy afternoon I like nothing better than losing myself in a good novel: I enjoy the colors, scents, and tastes of this imaginary world. ☐

2. When playing language games, I'm strong in recalling words and combinations we've already used. ☐

3. I'm good at making small talk and keeping people entertained when conversation begins to flag. ☐

4. Unless I'm very tired or upset, I'm generally good at holding my attention on a task. ☐

5. I am strong at planning a project step by step. ☐

6. I've sometimes been told I'm a little literal-minded and miss people's intended meaning. ☐

7. I'm good at seeing the best way to fit things into a confined space like a refrigerator or a closet. ☐

8. In solving a problem, I rely on logic and reasoning. ☐

9. If I'm on a citybreak holiday in a new place, I'd rather rely on my sense of direction and on landmarks than bother with a map. ☐

10. When I'm dining out with friends, I'm the one people ask to work out how to split the restaurant bill. ☐

THE PUZZLES

The fifty brain games that follow test the types of thinking typically associated with left-brain or right-brain processing.

You are the navigator: On the basis of how well you do on the questions, and how easy you find them, plot your own way through the book. If you're proving strong in right-brain thinking, turn to questions that develop typically left-brain skills—and vice versa: The aim is to develop a balanced, mature thinking style. Look out for thinking tips on each page to stimulate your approach and promote effective mental performance … and for explanations and further tips in the answer section from page 75 onward. None of this should be hard work: The puzzles are designed to intrigue and deliver the fulfillment of a challenge overcome. Be alert to developments in your performance levels and in how confident you feel about different types of thinking—and enjoy!

(Turn to page 9 if you need a reminder of how to score yourself as you progress through the book.)

Iris and Electra

One of the gimmicks with new cop show *Iris and Electra* is that the eponymous leads—Greek-American female cops in Chicago—are both mad on brain games and leave puzzles in the squad car for one another.

Here's Electra's latest grid: Can you place the numbers in the empty triangles so that the total of the six numbers in each hexagon is 25? Use only single digits between 1 and 9, and no two numbers in any hexagon can be the same.

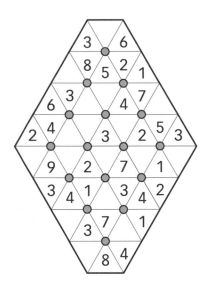

THINKING TIP
Focus on the process of what you are doing; don't get distracted thinking about the end product or the result.

On the Wild Side

UFO enthusiast, crop-circle obsessive, and potter January Skelton devises this intriguing puzzle—a New Age recombination of geometrical shapes found in crop circles—for her seafront store, On the Wild Side. Can you solve it?

Study the relationship between A and B and select the figure below that has the same relationship to C.

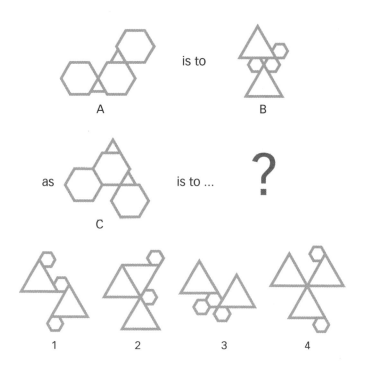

is to

A   B

as   is to ...   **?**

C

1   2   3   4

THINKING TIP
If you manage to focus on the process of what you're doing (see tip opposite), this helps you to avoid feeling impatient or worried about the outcome. Anxiety can be a major cause of poor mental performance.

Gold Affair

Ph.D. student Aaron finds this intriguing puzzle among the papers of renowned novelist Benjamin Gold. Recognizing the handwriting of Gold's secret lover, mathematician Anna Horvatz, Aaron is thrilled to discover more evidence of this little-known love affair. It will add spice to his upcoming biography of the great writer.

Anna's challenge is this: The four points are the corners of a square; the coordinates for A are (3, 9) and for C are (8, 2)—what are the coordinates of the other two points? To find the answer, start by plotting a grid …

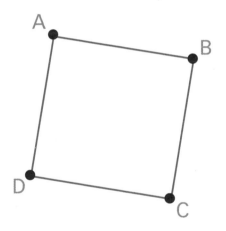

THINKING TIP
Your thinking may benefit from making an effort to broaden your horizons—for starters, seek out overseas news or read books from foreign cultures.

I-man Malfunction

Portrait painter Joy is in the unusual position of needing to help her studio robot, I-man, with a start-up malfunction. To get I-man going she has to complete the grid so that every row and column, and every outlined area, contains all of the symbols. Can you help Joy sort it out?

				Ø	
Σ	∞		¥		π	Ø
	Ω			Σ		
			Ω		¥	
Ø	Σ			¥		Ω
			∞		Σ	ð
	π	Σ				∞

THINKING TIP
Important task coming up? Listen to music first. Doing so has been shown to promote the release of the neurotransmitter dopamine in parts of the brain that govern close attention.

85 Degrees in the Shade

Time can drag for the waiters at the beach café. On a slow day, Alain sketches this placement grid puzzle: Can you solve it? Every chair has one parasol found horizontally or vertically adjacent to it. No parasol can be in a square next to another one (even diagonally). The numbers by each row and column tell you how many parasols there are—can you find the other nine?

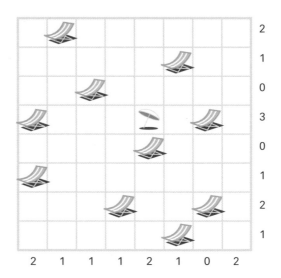

THINKING TIP
Making sure you get enough sleep is a key way to improve mental performance. Long-term sleep disruption damages neurons in brain areas linked to alertness.

Black Ship Docking

In a sci-fi movie version of Homer's *The Odyssey*, spaceman Hud Ysseus has to complete the sequence before he can bring his spacecraft *The Black Ship* in to dock. Can you help him? Look for the pattern in the sequence and work out what comes next from the five options.

1   2   3   4   5

THINKING TIP
Try to make time in your schedule for relaxation and games—if possible, use your imagination. Neuroscientists report that imaginative play boosts the growth in connections among neurons in your brain's frontal lobe.

Iris Pattern

Here's another numbergrid from Iris and Electra (see page 18). Each square in the grid needs to be filled with a single-digit number from 1–9, and each of those numbers is used four times. Use the clues to complete the grid, bearing in mind that the same number must not appear in two adjacent (touching) squares either across or down (diagonal is fine). If the same number is used more than once in any row or column, this is stated in the clue.

Across:

1 Two fives. No even numbers.

2 Two twos. No three. No five.

3 Total thirty-nine.

4 Two nines. Two threes.

5 Three ones.

6 Two eights. No two.

Down:

1 Two threes. No even numbers.

2 No seven.

3 Six consecutive numbers, placed in ascending order.

4 No six.

5 Two nines.

6 Total twenty-one.

THINKING TIP
Make an effort to seek mental stimulation through the new and unexpected. Perhaps surprisingly, research shows that using the internet typically makes us more insular and set in our ways.

Naviback

Sailing school proprietor Conrad Redd devises this backward-navigation exercise for his beginner pupils. In the exercise, each of the four styles of ball represents a different direction—north, south, east, or west. Moving from ball to adjacent ball either vertically or horizontally, plot a path that visits every ball and ends on the black one. What is the first ball on your trip?

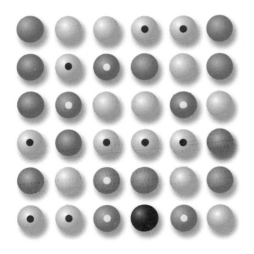

THINKING TIP
Aim for the simple. It's a productive discipline to state problems and solutions in the simplest possible terms.

YOUR
SCORE

LEFT-BRAIN PUZZLE 5   Level 1

Maxwell's Graduation

In 2049, all the students in Maxwell's final-year class have to win a game of Boxes—without help from their online tutors—before being allowed to graduate.

In the game, each player takes turns in joining two dots. If the line completes a box, you get another go straightaway. Maxwell's up against a cyber-opponent, Cecilia. Can you help him? What move will give Cecilia the least number of boxes on her next turn?

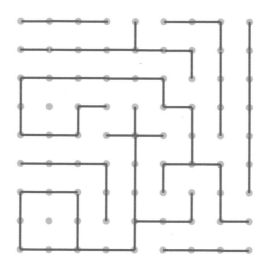

YOUR
SCORE

26

A@A

In New Orleans, Allyson and Antoine are opening a web design consultancy: A@A. This puzzle is sent out with their promotional material. Which of the four @ options below should take the place of the question mark?

   ?

1   2   3   4

THINKING TIP
Try to become aware of habitual faults in your mental performance: Do you regularly misread or overlook fine detail? Are you reluctant to change direction once committed to something, even if the evidence suggests you should?

Tree of Knowledge

Science teacher Doris devised this puzzle for the school fete. Choose one letter per leaf and unscramble them to decipher the surnames of three famous scientists. There will be unused letters (from the leaves with two): These will spell out the surname of another renowned scientist.

1 Born in Germany, this physicist developed the general theory of relativity and wrote the formula $E = MC^2$.

2 Hailing from England, this mathematician formulated the laws of motion and universal gravity.

3 This Greek philosopher, a student of Plato, was one of the first true scientists and tutor to Alexander the Great.

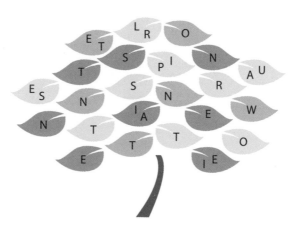

THINKING TIP
Analogies can be a key tool when you're solving a puzzle or thinking through a problem. What is this situation like? Can I get a fresh insight by trying to view this challenge from a different perspective?

Break-in at Lily-Rose's

Sharp-eyed private eye Lloyd Kane has noticed that you need only four of the six available pieces to patch up the stained-glass window broken by burglars in chanteuse Lily-Rose's apartment. Which four of the six parts do you need?

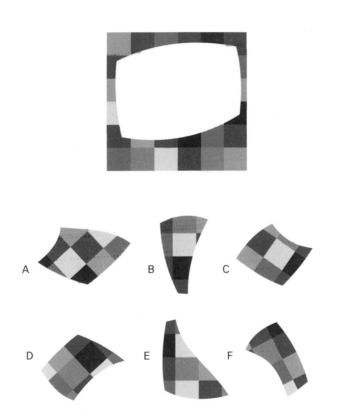

YOUR SCORE

LEFT-BRAIN PUZZLE 7   Level 3

Figure It In

Personal trainer Jessa adds mental workouts to her physical fitness regime. Can you fit all of the numbers below into her grid?

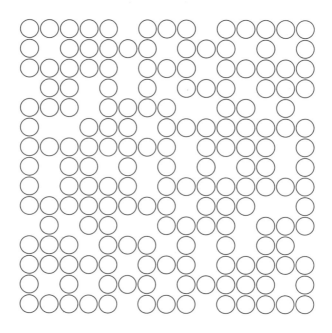

2 digits	357	4 digits	5 digits	6 digits	8 digits
13	453	1341	27809	199023	17679110
45	471	3211	30436	265684	20226154
68	519	3395	31989	482020	65560344
89	520	4235	37340	537086	72482914
90	589	4695	40704	567997	
94	590	4905	41843	588569	
	627	5413	53190		
3 digits	646	6142	63541	7 digits	
138	710	6573	71684	1365612	
159	739	7346	72116	2246147	
271	800	8085	73204	2749425	
282	807	8769	82808	6003427	
299	814	9562	90537	7064983	
353		9730	98686		

YOUR SCORE

30

Manhattan Mix-up

Three girls—Shoshanna, Marie, and Abi—catch a taxi on a night out in NYC. The ride comes to $25, so they each give the driver $10 and tell him to keep a $2 tip. He hands them back $1 each and keeps $2 for himself. The girls have paid $9 each, the cab driver has $2.

$27 + $2 = $29 ... What happened to the other dollar?

THINKING TIP
Sometimes you need to make a lateral-thinking shift to see around what seems logically impossible. Choosing random not regular can spark new perspectives ... pick a book in an unfamiliar genre, take a new route—do the unexpected!

More or Less

Yoga in the mathematics faculty: Teacher Hieronymus Sloan gives his pupils a "brain blast" warm-up before they start on their exercise. The task: Find a path from the top black button to the bottom one. Each sum on the path must give an answer that is 1 more or 1 less than the previous sum. No pen or pencil— mental math only!

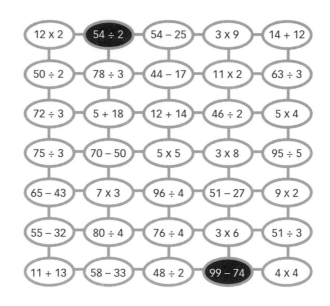

THINKING TIP
Remember the value of asking "Why?" Check you're clear on your own aims. It's also a valuable strategy to interrogate other people's motives and to consider why a person is doing something in a particular way or at a particular time.

Unify

Brother Marcus has visions of himself climbing upward over great blocks during his hour of meditation at the monastery. He is inspired to make this simple block puzzle toy to raise money for the local food bank.

Which two of Marcus's block groups could be fitted neatly together to make a perfect 3x3x3 cube?

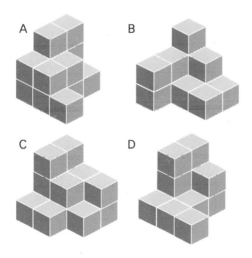

A   B

C   D

THINKING TIP
Make sure you're open to the possibility that you may be wrong. This can greatly improve your decision-making.

YOUR
SCORE

Ant It a Shame

A picnic mishap: Ants in the sugar means that Bharati cannot enjoy her tea sweetened as she likes. But it inspires her to devise this simple puzzle for her mathematics class.

Here is the challenge: The ant has been on a journey, visiting every one of the twenty sugar cubes. Can you trace back her trip and work out where it started?

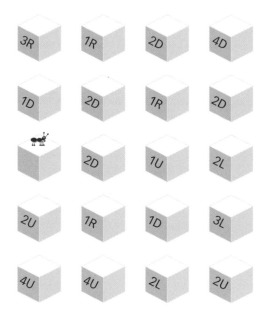

THINKING TIP
In thinking and putting the results of thought into action, give the utmost care to choosing the right means to the end you have selected.

Blue Period

After math whiz Benjamin Blue is laid off by the university, his brother Sammy persuades him to help out on the mother of all art heists. The boys (dressed as IT technicians) have to make it through the outer gallery to lift the artwork—a Blue Period Picasso—and then make their way out through the same gallery with their prize. Can you help them make it from A to B through the museum and out from B to A again? On the way in, avoid any security guards with sunglasses. Coming out, avoid the cops!

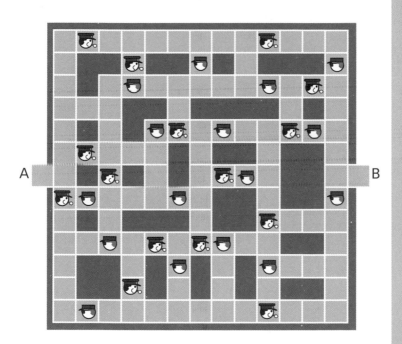

THINKING TIP
Keep an eye on your state of mind, which tends to condition your thinking. Are your emotions merely reflecting those of people around you?

Tab's Tailor Trial

On his first day as tailor's apprentice, Tab is given a challenge: Four boxes made of different metals contain different-colored buttons. Each box has three different quantities of three colors; so the box with fourteen blue buttons, say, doesn't have fourteen green or fourteen red buttons. How many of each in every box?

1 The silver box contains one more blue button than the gold box, more green buttons than the copper box, and two more red buttons than the tin box.

2 There are more blue buttons in the copper box than there are red buttons in the gold box.

3 The box with the fewest blue buttons contains two more green buttons than there are in the box with fifteen red buttons.

	Blue				Green				Red			
	12	13	14	15	13	14	15	16	12	14	15	17
Copper box												
Gold box												
Silver box												
Tin box												
Red 12												
14												
15												
17												
Green 13												
14												
15												
16												

Box	Blue	Green	Red

THINKING TIP
Don't immediately dismiss ideas that seem impossible. This is something we can learn from children, who are much more open in their thinking.

Art's Ark

Brainstorming stage designs for a new musical based on Noah's Ark, Art Ransome sketches out this puzzle. Can you draw walls to partition the grid into areas so that each area contains two animals (represented by squares)? Area sizes must match those shown below the grid and each + must be linked to at least two walls.

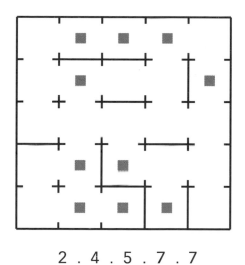

2 . 4 . 5 . 7 . 7

THINKING TIP
Deep down, we all have an evolutionary drive to master challenges. It's worth making a deliberate effort to learn from setbacks and difficulties—try asking, how could I vary my approach another time?

On the Grid

Mathematics graduate Adam founds taxi firm On the Grid and hires as many overqualified unemployed graduates as he can to be drivers. One gimmick is the provision of math materials for passengers to enjoy during the ride. If you can complete this 9x9 sudoku before the end of your ride (let's say, 10 minutes), you'll pay no fare.

Standard sudoku rules apply: Place the numbers 1–9 once in each row, column, and 3x3 box in the grid. In addition, numbers around the outside give the sum of the numbers in the first/last three squares in the respective row/column.

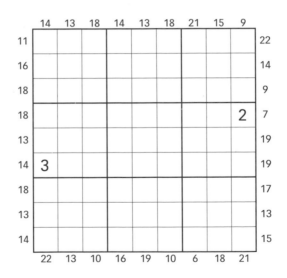

THINKING TIP
Practice using fully focused attention on tasks—even housework or other mundane activities. Nothing is really boring if you pay full attention. With practice you can improve your concentration.

Five Hands Five

An unlikely combination—an opera about poker: In *Five Hands Five*, experimental composer Harald Hudson dramatizes the adventures of prim English poker ace Polly Queen in Vegas. In this game, issued to promote the production, Polly's opponent has a five-card poker hand with all the cards being either 10, Jack, Queen, King, or Ace. She has five guesses.

To the left of each guess, a white dot indicates there is a card of the right suit in the wrong place, while a black dot means a card of the right suit in the right place. To the right, a white dot indicates a card of the right value in the wrong place and a black dot means a card of the right value in the right place. The gray dots on either side indicate cards with the wrong suit/value and placement. What's the hand?

THINKING TIP
Don't be afraid to go out on a limb sometimes. Timidity can be a great disadvantage in thinking.

YOUR
SCORE

Cecilia's Challenge

Back to 2049 (see page 26): A significantly more difficult version of Maxwell's high-school graduation puzzle is used to test under-graduates passing out from their online training programs. As before, in this game each player takes turns in joining two dots. If the line completes a box, you get another go straightaway. Like Maxwell, the teachers are playing against cyber-opponent Cecilia. What move will give Cecilia the least number of boxes on her next turn?

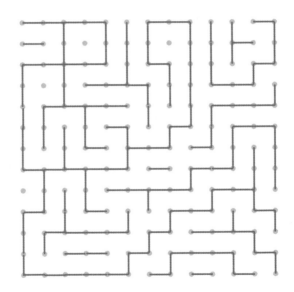

THINKING TIP
As your concentration improves (see tip on page 38), you'll be more fully engaged with each task and less distracted by doubts and fears about your performance or what other people will think of you.

A Philosophical Handyman

On the first day of his new job maintaining an office building, handyman and philosophy graduate Sam Beckett is inundated with complaints about the three vending machines in the lobby. Each machine is labeled and dispenses one drink—but all three machines are dispensing a drink that doesn't match the label. Tea, coffee, and soup are available, but not from the correct machines. Using just one token, can you help Sam relabel the machines correctly?

THINKING TIP
Be willing to embrace contradictions. This can lead you to rare and valuable new insights.

DD's Appointment

Undercover operative Thomas "Desmond" Dekker—codename DD—has been sent this time sequence puzzle on the understanding that he will work out the time on the fifth clock—the time of his appointment with his minder, Z, at Waterloo Station, in London. Can you help him? At what time should DD head to Waterloo?

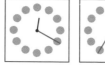

1   2   3   4   5

THINKING TIP
Make an effort to shake things up: Don't let the horizons of your thinking be set by what you have thought to be right for a long time.

"Happy Happy"

Promoter and nightclub owner Harlow Bennett installs this touch-sensitive floor in the new "Happy Happy" room at his club Newcycle. Starting at the top-left face, dancers move horizontally or vertically from face to face to reach the bottom-right face— without ever passing through consecutive faces with the same expression. Can you make it across? Free tropical juice spritzer for those who can make the "journey" in less than 2 minutes!

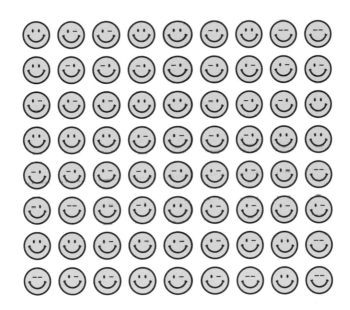

THINKING TIP
Treat received wisdom with caution.

YOUR
SCORE

Dr. Donald Explores

Crash-landing on a previously unknown planet, space-age anthropologist Dr. Daniel Donald discovers an abandoned hi-tech university apparently dedicated to the glories of mathematics. He encounters this number square at the entrance to the inner sanctum. Can you help Dr. Donald complete the number square so that the numbers 1–25 are all in the grid, and all rows and columns add up to the totals indicated to the right and below?

9					43
10		7	23		85
	16	13		4	53
11	15		22	20	76
	14	12			68
65	94	46	55	65	

THINKING TIP
Don't forget to consider what is missing. Looking at the statement of a problem, remember to think about what may have been left out and what is not immediately visible.

Sunetrart

Artist Sunetra aims to brings the random into her monochrome "Sunetrart" poster designs by asking her husband Jared, a mathematician, to design number-shade puzzles like this.

This is how to fill in the design: Shade in certain cells, so that every number in the puzzle is part of a continuous unshaded area containing the stated number of cells. There must be precisely one number per unshaded area, and unshaded areas cannot touch horizontally or vertically (only diagonally). Shaded cells cannot form any solid 2x2 (or larger) areas. Additionally, all shaded cells must form one continuous area (touching at the corners of cells counts).

3		2		2		4			
	8			4				
					6			4	
			3		3		2		3

THINKING TIP
Setting time limits for tasks can help aid focus. If you have a long piece of work or a very complex problem, working in several short bursts with breaks in between can be more productive than applying yourself nonstop for several hours.

"Bardo Steps"

In the new video game "Bardo Steps," players find themselves in an unfamiliar reality after experiencing physical death. The first task is to engage with this directional problem to find their way to Welcome Temple. These are the rules: Every oval in the diagram should contain a different letter of the alphabet from A to K. Use the clues below to determine their locations. (References to "due west," "due north," and so on indicate any position along one horizontal or vertical line.)

1 The A is due south of the B and due west of the C (which is farther north than the D).

2 The E is due south of the F and farther east than the G (which is farther north than the H).

3 The I is due east of the D and due north of the J (which is farther south than the E).

4 The H is due south of the I and due east of the K.

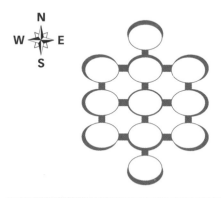

THINKING TIP
Try gaming. Video games can be good for your thinking. Research in 2013 showed that playing these games boosts concentration and spatial ability.

Sir Christopher's Chess Position

Retired British civil servants Sir Christopher and Sir Terry have played chess since they were at school 70 years ago. These days when they meet they swap chess problems like this rather than playing the game. Here's one of Sir Christopher's best examples. He asks Sir Terry: Can you place a queen, a bishop, a knight, and a rook on this chessboard so that the marked squares are attacked by exactly two pieces, three pieces, or four pieces?

Remember: The queen can move any number of squares, in any direction; the bishop can move any number of squares, but diagonally only; the knight moves in an L shape, two squares in one direction then one at a right angle; and the rook can move any number of squares, forward, backward, and to the sides (but not diagonally). In this puzzle, all of the pieces can jump over the numbered squares.

 THINKING TIP
We need self-confidence to act and think freely and independently. But if we are overconfident, we may not be thinking at all—only telling ourselves that we are right, or that we already know what we need to know.

YOUR SCORE

I-chef Crisis

Joy has a kitchen robot, I-chef, as well as her studio helper I-man (see page 21). But I-chef's operating system has crashed while he's preparing a five-course dinner for Joy's agent and several important clients. She needs to reboot him as quickly as possible. Can you help? Determine which nine of the fourteen statements below are true and which five are false. For false responses, shade in the corresponding areas on the reboot interface—the remaining unshaded areas will display a two-number combination to restart I-chef.

A 289 is a cube

B A heptagon has six sides

C 123 + 321 = 444

D 10 million has eight zeros

E 4,356 ÷ 44 = 99

F 17 is a factor of 221

G 1 x 2 x 3 x 4 x 5 = 120

H 4.5 x 54 = 243

I 777 is a third of 2231

J Half of 246,912 is 123,456

K 44 x 55 = 2,440

L DLV is 555 in Roman numerals

M Pi times 6 is less than 20

N 31 is the square root of 1,089

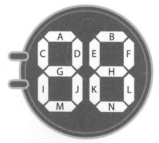

THINKING TIP
Try thinking in opposites. You may think of silk as soft, a pure luxury; but did you know that silk can be fashioned into screws? And that silk screws are strong enough to be used in binding broken bones?

Crop Circle Abstract

Here is another of potter and UFO enthusiast January Skelton's puzzles based on crop circle shapes for her On the Wild Side shop (see page 19). She uses these five shapes, one each, on a set of five cups, plates, and bowls in her Celestial Connections range. Which one of the five below is not part of a pair and is therefore the odd one out?

B

A

C

E

D

YOUR
SCORE

49 Dogs in the Bedroom

Rosalind devised this puzzle for her boyfriend Benny, a professional dogwalker, on the day that he got his 49th client. A miniaturist artist, she painted the grid in ink on their bedroom wall. The task is to complete the grid, starting at 1 and filling in all the missing numbers up to 49 so that they connect consecutively either horizontally, vertically, or diagonally in any direction.

				21		
	1	23	13		19	
	28					16
30		41		43	11	
31	40		4		49	9
	34	35			8	
				7		

THINKING TIP
Do you struggle to concentrate? Try meditation. It has proven capacity to improve concentration.

Honeycomb at "Sphere"

Designer Rodger creates a slot-together honeycomb table in monochrome for his pal Sammy McLintock's jazz club "Sphere." The manufacturer has delivered three correct sections and one incorrect one. Can you spot one section among the four below that does not belong in the main table? The pieces may be rotated as necessary.

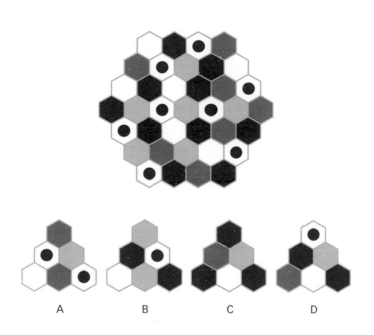

A   B   C   D

THINKING TIP
The seeds of a solution are often found in the problem. Physicist Niels Bohr reportedly said: "Every great and deep difficulty bears in itself its own solution. It forces us to change our thinking in order to find it."

YOUR SCORE

Floodwater Panic

The floodwaters are rising and they say the river is threatening to burst its banks. But restaurant owner Ruchir's security system has chosen today to malfunction. He has to select the correct numbergrid from the four at the bottom to override the security system so he can manually raise the flood defenses in his basement and storerooms.

Can you help him? First, study the relationship between X and Y, then decide which grid below has the same relationship to Z.

X

4	7	9	6
3	7	1	4
5	1	2	5
7	5	3	8

is to

Y

3	6	1	3
5	0	2	4
7	4	3	7
4	6	9	5

as

Z

5	2	1	3
4	2	8	4
7	4	9	6
8	5	0	7

is to ...

A

2	5	2	0
7	1	3	4
9	7	4	9
1	7	3	2

B

4	1	0	2
3	1	7	4
6	3	8	5
7	4	9	6

C

4	1	3	1
5	2	5	4
4	4	6	8
2	5	7	0

D

4	1	8	3
7	3	9	5
8	4	0	6
5	1	1	2

YOUR
SCORE

THINKING TIP
Emotion can be an enemy of clear thinking. Practicing being aware of your emotions can help you control the anger or frustration that might overwhelm your reasoning.

Maurice Moves On

Crooked businessman Maurice is playing a cat-and-mouse game with Amit and the serious-fraud investigators who are on his case. One step ahead of Amit, he's grabbed all his cash and has left his trademark signature in the empty office safe: fourteen cards arranged in a pattern as shown, with the fifteenth stuck face down on the base of the safe.

By studying the pattern, can you work out the value and suit of the fifteenth card? It's a clue intended to give two elements of the map coordinates for where he's gone into hiding.

THINKING TIP

A key part of thinking can be knowing when to stop pondering, make a decision, and press forward. Napoleon Bonaparte reputedly said: "Take time to deliberate, but when the time for action has arrived, stop thinking and go in."

YOUR
SCORE

The Loop

Experimental filmmaker Grayson Green uses this puzzle as the centerpiece of his movie *Square*. Step by step, characters solve the puzzle while around them an espionage plot plays out. The requirements of the puzzle: You must draw a single loop using horizontal and vertical lines only, and the loop must not pass through any cell more than once; any cell the loop does not visit must be shaded in. No shaded cells can touch in either a horizontal or vertical direction. Numbers with arrows (clue squares) indicate how many shaded cells appear in a given direction in a specific row or column; clue squares should be left untouched and do not form part of the loop, nor are they to be shaded in. Not all shaded cells are necessarily identified with arrows.

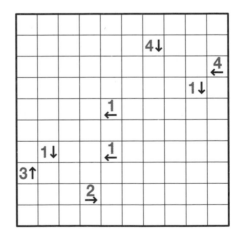

THINKING TIP
Confidence in your ability with numbers will help you make quick decisions and think on your feet, so it's worth practicing simple arithmetic from day to day. Don't rely on your calculator. Use your brain.

Temple Wall

Anthropologist Barney Weiss makes the discovery of a lifetime when a freak tidal event uncovers a centuries-old temple complex previously lost beneath deep sand: The group of miraculously preserved buildings is centered on a temple with a wall design as shown below. Curiously, one piece is missing from the design, but five loose panels (A–E) are found below. Barney sets to work to determine which of the panels should complete the design.

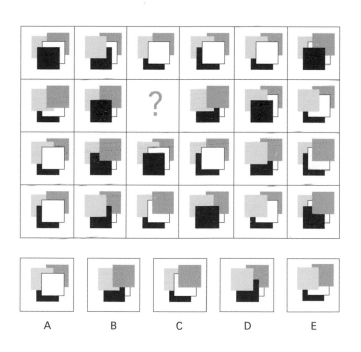

A   B   C   D   E

THINKING TIP
If you get stuck, don't give up, but don't plug on and on, either. Take a break, then return to it later. Stephen Hawking said: "What I do is keep thinking about the problem but work on something else. Sometimes it is years before I see the way forward."

YOUR
SCORE

Thunder Path

Downstairs at the blues club, puzzle-loving guitarist Albert "The Storm" Thunder opens this brain game in a letter from his son Marvin. Here's the challenge: Form a path through the grid that starts in the top-left corner and finishes in the bottom-right. Numbers must link together in the order 1–2–3–4 and then back to 1 again. The path may cross over itself, and may move horizontally, vertically, or diagonally, but must visit every number in the grid only once.

1	4	3	2	4	2	3	4
3	2	1	4	1	3	1	2
2	3	4	1	1	2	4	3
1	3	2	4	2	3	1	4
2	4	3	1	1	3	1	3
1	3	4	2	2	4	2	4
4	3	2	1	1	2	2	1
2	1	4	3	4	3	3	4

THINKING TIP
Are you seeing things clearly? Consider whether you're reading a situation accurately. Mistakes in thinking and decision-making can often result from failures of perception.

King for the Day

Here's one of the challenges on new TV game show *King for the Day*. One of a dozen cakes is a King Cake, containing a gold coin that will make you King for the Day. Using a weighing scale three times only, can you find the King Cake?

THINKING TIP
When forming opinions, don't rely on one source or on sources all of one kind. Get the other side's view.

Lauren's Lucky Five

Retired teachers Lauren Lewis and Madeleine Fabre play the Lotto religiously. Lauren also devises Lotto-themed puzzles for her friend to keep her alert in their retirement complex. So here's Lauren's puzzle for Madeleine this week: Can you find the lucky five from this clue—none of the five winning balls is black, contains the number four, or is divisible by seven?

THINKING TIP
When you're considering a problem at work or college, check from time to time to see how well you're concentrating. Use this time to refocus.

Party Like It's 2099

Los Angeles, New Year's Eve 2099: Movie director and wine connoisseur Ephraim "Sam" Goldwyn needs to align seven hexagons to open his wine cellar in order to seek out some rare Bordeaux vintages for his guests. Can you help him? Rotate the seven hexagons until all the neighboring panels match up.

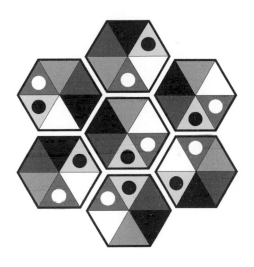

THINKING TIP
Another key aspect of checking your focus (see the thinking tip opposite) is to make sure that you are addressing the question and not allowing yourself to be sidelined into a parallel (or even irrelevant) issue.

Beachgrid

Mathematician Asa takes a job selling tickets for deckchairs on the beach. In hard sand at the back of the beach he sketches this numbergrid. Can you solve it? The task is to place numbers in the empty triangles so that the total of the six numbers in each hexagon is 30. Use only single digits between 1 and 9, and no two numbers in any hexagon can be the same.

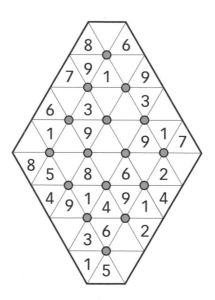

THINKING TIP
Daydreaming can have benefits—especially if you're in need of insight to solve an intractable problem.

They Walked Free

In WW2 prison camp movie *They Walked Free*, Camp Commandant Heinrich Baum intercepts this communication, which he believes is sending the date and time of a planned escape. Can you determine what should occupy the squares at A, B, and C to crack the code before him and help the prisoners escape?

5	3		5	7		
	3	4	3		9	1
		A		8	1	9
4			B	4	4	
1	9	7		C	3	
1		4	4	1	3	7
9	5	3				3

THINKING TIP
Value your natural curiosity. Try to make the most of it in everything you do.

"Archipelago"

In the video game "Archipelago," eccentric British explorer Sir Jasper Buckingham is marooned on a series of islands. Reaching Level 2 of the game, Caleb has to solve this island-bridging challenge. Connect every island (represented by circles) into a single interconnected group. To do this, draw bridges between islands. The number in each circle states how many bridges must be connected to that island. Bridges cannot cross each other, can only be drawn horizontally or vertically, and there can be a maximum of two bridges between any pair of islands.

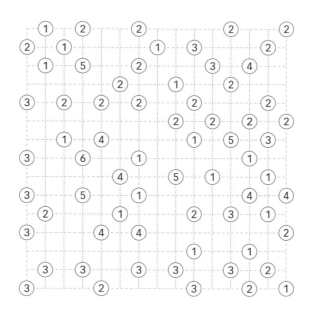

THINKING TIP
Comparing a challenge with previous problems and solutions can be a useful approach. Could I use the strategy I used that time? How is today's problem similar to or different from yesterday's?

Chez Alexandre

Restaurateur Alexandre wants his café in the university area to have changing wall designs. He asks his friend, artist Fabienne, to create numbered grids that produce different shaded designs when finished. Can you complete this one?

Shade in the cells in such a way that every number in the puzzle is part of a continuous unshaded area containing the stated number of cells. There must be precisely one number per unshaded area and unshaded areas cannot touch horizontally or vertically (only diagonally). Shaded cells cannot form any solid 2x2 (or larger) areas. Additionally, all shaded cells must form one continuous area (touching at the corners of cells counts).

15							9
	5						
		5					
	15						
	4						

THINKING TIP
Seek feedback and advice. We can all benefit from the input of other people into our thinking and planning. Co-workers or friends may spot errors you have overlooked or bring a new perspective on a problem.

YOUR
SCORE

Sudocrew

To attract youth off the streets in the inner-city area where he lives, local boy and math professor Juan Carlos starts a youth drop-in club offering recreational math alongside other attractions such as ping-pong and indoor soccer. His "Sudocrew" is a club for young women and men who prove themselves adept with numbers. To join, you have to complete five overlapping sudoku grids: Place the numbers from 1–9 once in each of the rows, columns, and 3x3 boxes that make up the five individual grids.

YOUR SCORE

THINKING TIP
Don't be afraid to identify and question assumptions lying behind information or the manner in which it is presented.

Interlock

For her lonely hearts website, Interlock, Käthe devises this puzzle: Just like two people in a successful relationship, the horizontal and vertical elements interlock in a way that allows both difference and unity. Which whole-number value should be given to each symbol in order to reach the total shown at the end of each row? (Empty squares have no value.) And which whole-number value should be given to each symbol in order to reach the total shown at the base of each column? The number given to each symbol in the columns may differ from that given to each symbol in the rows.

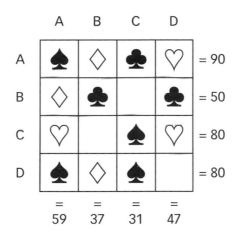

THINKING TIP
Take your time. This helps you to hold your full attention on what you are doing.

Reaching 9

In his workshop, bicycle builder Carter Phillips (see Thinking Challenge 1) likes to work through left-brain logic puzzles when he's taking a break. His girlfriend Rebecca made him this Reaching 9 puzzle to celebrate nine months together. Place the digits 1–9 in the grid so that it is possible to jump from one digit to the next, in order, using the steps provided in the diamonds on the right (for example, the 1,2 in the diamond one from the bottom on the left indicates one step left and two steps down). Each step must be used once, and some refer to numbers already placed. Both parts of a step must be used but can be taken in any order. No part of a step can travel over a black square.

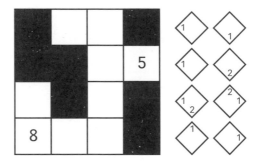

THINKING TIP
Try to stay calm and detached when people praise you and your work. This will help you cope if you are also criticized.

Polly's Aria

In Act 3 of Harald Hudson's poker opera *Five Hands Five* (see page 39), Polly Queen performs an exquisite aria while she solves this plot challenge: Her opponent Homer Ryan has a five-card poker hand with all the cards being either 10, Jack, Queen, King, or Ace. She has five guesses. As before, to the left of each guess, a white dot indicates a card of the right suit in the wrong place, while a black dot means a card of the right suit in the right place. To the right, a white dot indicates a card of the right value in the wrong place and a black dot means a card of the right value in the right place. The gray dots indicate cards with the wrong value and placement. What's the hand?

	Q♦	10♦	J♥	Q♣	10♣	
○○●●●	K♦	K♠	J♦	A♦	10♣	○○○○○
○○●○○						●●●○○
○○●●●	A♠	Q♥	K♣	A♠	J♠	●●○○○
○○○●●	A♦	K♦	Q♦	10♣	J♣	●●○○○
○○○○●	J♠	A♥	A♦	K♠	10♥	●○○○○

THINKING TIP
Check regularly that you are keeping your aim and audience in mind.

THINKING CHALLENGE 2

Try this next thinking challenge to make a second assessment of your left-brain/right-brain thinking styles, and to determine to what extent you have managed to bring balance to your thinking in working through this book.

You're back on the riverboat with a group of Maharaja guests (see pages 12–14), and the swell of the water is worse than before. This time you don't feel seasick. But you're tired and feel under the weather: You stagger a little and your hand bangs the side of the boat. At once the words "Are you sure you want to quit now?" hang strangely before your eyes. You say "No" firmly, and they disappear.

The explanation is that you're not really on a riverboat, you're sitting in a hard chair in a rather dingy office wearing a virtual-reality headset. You did so well in covering for your boss that you were offered a job at the Maharaja travel company, and have been working there for a full twelve months. Now you're taking part in a job assessment. This VR trial is part of your interview for a more senior position ...

"Summertime"

Today it's exactly one year on from your first day at Maharaja, and the same seven clients have all booked themselves in on a return visit because they had such a good experience first time round. (If it is some time since you worked through Thinking Challenge 1, you may want to turn back to pages 12–13 to refresh your memory of the key facts about the guests: Jonty Gerrard, Rebecca Mirviss, Nisha Cohen, Sir Charles Tattershall, Andrew Burns, Marco Cohen, and Carter Phillips. But read them through once only.)

It's a bright and sunny day in the simulation. The light bounces off the water as you prepare to greet the guests on the deck. Your first task is to deliver a short speech welcoming the travelers back and telling them about the treats you have in store. Perhaps you might start off with a few sentences that make reference to their specific areas of interest, being sure to mention them by name …

Notes

The date and time read-out in your field of vision states that it is Thursday, August 4, 2016, 10:45—you have just fifteen minutes before the riverboat is due to dock. Prior to that, your next task is to check a set of invoices from the riverboat company covering the last week's trips. You then have to settle the account, working out a tip of 7.5 percent of the total due to the riverboat captain. These are the figures:

- Friday, July 29—$400
- Saturday, July 30—$850
- Sunday, July 31—$325
- Monday, August 1—refund $205
- Tuesday, August 2—$375
- Wednesday, August 3—$725
- Thursday, August 4—$215

You frown with concentration. Your task is not made easier by the fact that in the background, Carter, Marco, and Andrew have become embroiled in a noisy but friendly debate over whether

Notes

Louis Armstrong's version of the song "Summertime" can match that of Billie Holliday!

Next you're told that staff preparing the dining area for the reception in the luxury dockside restaurant have walked out in an industrial dispute. It's up to you to do the decoration. Because this is a virtual-reality test, it is easy enough for you to change the colors and fittings of the décor in this very grand restaurant. To do this, you have to view the options on your smartphone and text through your choices. Not only that, you also have to devise the best way to present the food that has been prepared for the event by top chef Hugo …

When the riverboat docks and the guests are all safely ashore, you receive a new message: "A major accident on the freeway means that the limousines are unable to get through and there is no way of driving them to the Eden Hotel. Change of plan— guests are now booked in to the Red Fort Hotel." The trouble is, you are unfamiliar with this part of the town and you have

Notes

never traveled the route, details of which you now hear coming through your headphones:

From dock, left on Waterside Avenue; 200 yards to Louis Armstrong statue (you note this detail with interest!) *at junction with 9th Avenue; 100 yards straight to cycle taxi rank at junction with Market Stretch; 750 yards right along May Way to Ella's jazz club on October Street; left 500 yards opposite City Orchard to Green Fields Park and then cross this diagonally to the exit by the Elegance department store and 100 yards right on Green Quarter and on to new hotel, the Red Fort.*

So now you have to devise a way of getting your guests to the hotel or persuading them that traveling there via an unconventional means may be a good thing.

Any ideas how you could go about it? Your future chances of success with the company rely on your quick-thinking brain once again ...

Notes

THE ANSWERS

In this book, the answer section is essential not only for checking your responses but also for scoring and finding your way through our left-brain/right-brain question strands.

You may come to your answers by way of a moment of sudden insight deriving from right-brain activity or only after methodically working through all the possible solutions, left-brain style. After you have checked your answer, don't forget to score yourself according to whether you were correct and how easy you found the process (from 0 for very difficult and incorrect to 5 for very easy/correct). As noted on page 9, if you score 0, 1, or 2, indicating that you struggled to some extent, proceed to a puzzle of the same kind—for example, from L1 to L2; if you score 3, 4, or 5, indicating that you are quite at home with this kind of challenge, proceed to a puzzle of the opposite kind— for example, from L1 to R1. The book will build up your confidence by helping you improve your performance in areas you find difficult.

LEFT PUZZLE 1   Iris and Electra

The completed grid is shown right. Iris and
Electra's interest in math problems is not a
distraction in the show because the girls regularly
make use of their ability with numbers to outwit
criminals and solve crimes in Chicago. If you got
Electra's puzzle right and found it fairly easy to
complete, you are strong in typically left-brain
activities such as arithmetic and the careful
plotting of information. As explained on page 9, award yourself a mark
of 3, 4, or 5 if you got it right and found it easy—and proceed to R1.
If you found it hard, score 0, 1, or 2—this means you need more
practice in typically left-brain thinking: Proceed to L2.

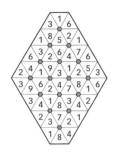

LEFT PUZZLE 2   Gold Affair

B is at (9, 8) and D is at (2, 3). You can find
the center of the square by averaging the
coordinates of A and C (5.5, 5.5) and working
out B and D from there.

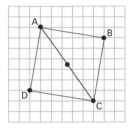

LEFT PUZZLE 3   85 Degrees in the Shade

The other nine parasols are shown on
Alain's grid, right. Combining numerical
logic and visual reasoning to plot
information on a grid in this way is a
typically left-brain strength. Film student
Alain, working at the café as a summer
job, is thrilled to find out that revered
Scandinavian director Søren Mikkelsen
is staying in the same resort and
sometimes comes to the café.

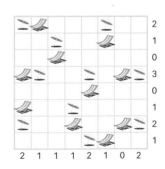

LEFT PUZZLE 4   Iris Pattern

The completed grid is shown right. Variety stimulates the brain, but in the modern world we sometimes need to make a deliberate effort to seek the unexpected. Ethan Zuckerman, director of the MIT Center for Civic Media, discusses how using the internet makes us more insular in his book *Rewire* (see page 95).

5	1	3	7	9	5
7	2	4	8	6	2
9	8	5	4	7	6
3	9	6	2	9	3
1	4	7	1	2	1
3	6	8	5	8	4

The internet may offer us access to perspectives from far-flung correspondents and to websites of newspapers in distant corners of the world, but we are typically more likely to focus on what is near and familiar, such as our friends' social media pages.

LEFT PUZZLE 5   Maxwell's Graduation

A vertical line to the left or right of the area shown will give up just one box to Maxwell's opponent. Could you see this?

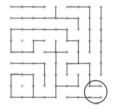

LEFT PUZZLE 6   Tree of Knowledge

1. Einstein; 2. Newton; 3. Aristotle. Tree of Knowledge answer: Louis PASTEUR. Doris tells her students that Einstein is the source of many enlightening ideas about thinking and mental processes. He reportedly noted: "We cannot solve our problems with the same thinking we used when we created them." It's a very good strategy, if you find yourself stuck with any problem, to consider a completely fresh approach.

LEFT PUZZLE 7   Figure It In

Jessa's grid should look as shown (right). Make a conscious effort to be open to unseen possibilities: If you are told, "There is no alternative" it can take strength of mind to resist. But you can greatly benefit your own and others' thinking by refusing to accept that.

```
6 3 5 4 1    4 5 3    2 7 8 0 9
2   3 7 3 4 0    3 5 7    0    7
7 2 1 1 6    7 3 9    4 1 8 4 3
  8 9    5    0    5 8 9    5 9 0
5 2 0    6 1 4 2    4 5    0
3    5 1 9    2 0 2 2 6 1 5 4
7 2 4 8 2 9 1 4    6 5 7 3    8
0    6 8    0    6    5    9 4    2
8    9 5 6 2    1 7 6 7 9 1 1 0
6 5 5 6 0 3 4 4    8 0 7    2
  4    9 0    7 3 4 6    7 1 0
8 1 4    3 5 3    1    4    1 3
7 3 2 0 4    2 9 9    9 8 6 8 6
6    3    2 7 1    8 2 8 0 8    4
9 0 5 3 7    1 5 9    3 0 4 3 6
```

LEFT PUZZLE 8   More or Less

The path and the answers to the sums are shown on the grid, right. It's of real benefit to practice mental math regularly. Confidence with numbers enhances your thinking.

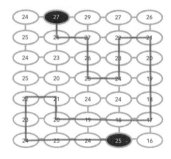

LEFT PUZZLE 9   Ant It a Shame

The ant's starting place is circled (see right), with its progress—sugar cube by cube—shown. With regard to means and ends (thinking tip, page 34): People often come unstuck by choosing to believe that the right end justifies a dubious means. But in fact, there is no way to the right end except through the right means, and choosing the right means is tantamount to achieving the end.

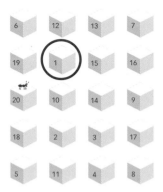

LEFT PUZZLE 10   Tab's Tailor Trial

Remember throughout that there are different quantities of the colors in each box (intro). There are either 12 or 15 red buttons in the tin box (clue 1). The box with 12 blue buttons hasn't 12 red buttons (intro) or 15 red buttons (clue 3), so the box with 12 blue buttons isn't tin. Nor is it silver (clue 1) or copper (clue 2), so 12 blue buttons are in the gold box and (clue 1) 13 blue buttons are in the silver box. The gold box thus hasn't 12 red buttons (intro), so (clue 2) the gold box has 14 red buttons and the copper box has 15 blue buttons. By elimination, the tin box has 14 blue buttons. The silver box has 17 red (clue 1) and the tin box 15 red. The copper box thus has 12 red. The tin box has 14 blue (above), so not 14 green (intro). Thus the tin box has 13 green (clue 3) and the gold box has 15 green. There are 16 green buttons in the silver box (clue 1) and 14 in the copper box. Thus:

- Copper box: 15 blue/14 green/12 red
- Gold box: 12 blue/15 green/14 red
- Silver box: 13 blue/16 green/17 red
- Tin box: 14 blue/13 green/15 red

LEFT PUZZLE 11 On the Grid

The completed grid is shown right. How was your timing? Does Adam owe you a free ride?

	14	13	18	14	13	18	21	15	9	
11	4	1	6	2	7	3	8	9	5	22
16	2	5	9	8	1	6	7	4	3	14
18	8	7	3	4	5	9	6	2	1	9
18	5	6	7	9	3	8	4	1	2	7
13	1	4	8	5	6	2	9	3	7	19
14	3	9	2	1	4	7	5	8	6	19
18	6	8	4	7	2	1	3	5	9	17
13	9	3	1	6	8	5	2	7	4	13
14	7	2	5	3	9	4	1	6	8	15
	22	13	10	16	19	10	6	18	21	

LEFT PUZZLE 12 Cecilia's Challenge

A line at the left or bottom of the marked square, right, will give up just one box to Cecilia. Students at the E-College of the mid-21st century have access to virtual dorms, libraries, and social areas.

LEFT PUZZLE 13 DD's Appointment

DD should head to Waterloo at 5:50. The clock is advancing by five minutes more each time, starting with a 75-minute move, then 80, 85, and 90. This puzzle relies on typically left-brain numerical thinking and logical analysis.

LEFT PUZZLE 14 Dr. Donald Explores

The completed grid should look as shown right. When Dr. Donald entered the final number, the large marble door beside the grid swung open to reveal a dark passage heading vertiginously downward. Dr. Donald fearlessly proceeded and far, far underground discovered what appeared to be a library with mathematical works inscribed in spidery writing on vellum.

9	25	6	2	1	43
10	24	7	23	21	85
17	16	13	3	4	53
11	15	8	22	20	76
18	14	12	5	19	68
65	94	46	55	65	

LEFT PUZZLE 15 "Bardo Steps"

The correct positions of the letters are as shown right. *Bardo* is a Tibetan word and refers to a concept in Tibetan Buddhism—that after your death you will go through an intermediate state (called the *bardo*) before being born again in a new physical setting. Players in the 21st century particularly enjoyed the game when using new virtual-reality headsets.

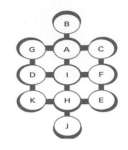

LEFT PUZZLE 16 I-chef Crisis

The reboot code is 54. The answers are:

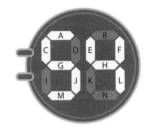

A True—of 17

B False—it has 7

C True

D False—it has seven zeros

E True

F True: 17 x 13 = 221

G True

H True

I False: 777 is a third of 2,331

J True

K False: 44 x 55 = 2,420

L True

M True

N False—33 is the square root of 1,089

LEFT PUZZLE 17 49 Dogs in the Bedroom

The completed grid looks as shown right. Forty-nine was a significant number for Benny's business because it was the target he had set himself when he started; he'd suggested fifty, but when Rosalind said that was too ambitious, he dropped by one. Meditation certainly helps develop

26	25	24	22	21	20	18
27	(1)	23	13	14	19	17
29	28	2	42	12	15	16
30	32	41	3	43	11	10
31	40	33	4	44	(49)	9
39	34	35	5	45	8	48
38	37	36	6	7	46	47

concentration (see page 50), but it has also been shown to make you thrive physically. Research in 2013 showed that meditation increases the activity of genes that boost good health.

LEFT PUZZLE 18 Floodwater Panic

D. In each column, each number has moved up one place (with the top number moving to the bottom), but 1 has also been removed from each number in the 2nd and 4th columns.

D

4	1	8	3
7	3	9	5
8	4	0	6
5	1	1	2

LEFT PUZZLE 19 The Loop

The completed puzzle is shown right. At the end of the movie it becomes clear that the characters' movements have followed the line of the loop as it would appear if the finished puzzle were overlaid on a map of Los Angeles.

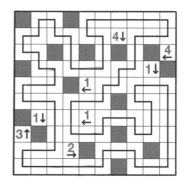

LEFT PUZZLE 20 Thunder Path

The path—starting from the 1 at top left and finishing with the 4 at bottom right—is shown on the grid, right. Though in his mid-seventies, Albert Thunder uses puzzles like this, which test and develop typically left-brain math and sequential processing, to help him keep mentally sharp and to enable him to focus before shows: "A little calm before the Storm," he jokes.

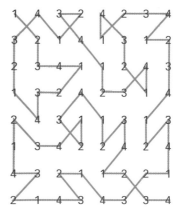

LEFT PUZZLE 21 Lauren's Lucky Five

The lucky five are 2, 8, 17, 23, and 38, as shown right—none contains 4, is divisible by 7, or is on a black ball as per the clue. If asked, Lauren, a former math teacher, will say that she is a left-brain analytical thinker but that Madeleine, who taught fine art and sculpture, is more of a right-brain type, who benefits from the workout provided by these sorts of puzzles.

LEFT PUZZLE 22 Beachgrid

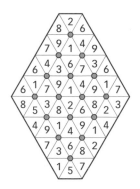

The completed grid should look as shown right, with each hexagon totaling 30. Asa has the summer of his life at the beach, not least because he meets and falls in love with his future wife, theology student Franseza, who is working at a seafront café. His chat-up line is that he shares a name not only with the founder of Coca-Cola (Asa Griggs Candler) but also with Al Jolson. Jolson's real name was Asa Yoelson.

LEFT PUZZLE 23 "Archipelago"

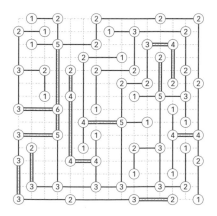

The completed Archipelago grid should look as shown right, with all the islands connected by bridges.

LEFT PUZZLE 24 Sudocrew

Here's the completed Sudocrew grid. Juan Carlos was impatient with people implying that the young people of the area wouldn't be interested in math and logic puzzles, but even he was surprised by the number of youths who applied to the Sudocrew and then stayed in it, taking pleasure in the problems and brain games he provided.

Top-left block:
4	6	7	1	3	8	2	5	9
2	3	1	6	9	5	4	8	7
8	9	5	4	7	2	3	6	1
6	7	9	5	4	3	1	2	8
1	4	3	8	2	6	7	9	5
5	8	2	9	1	7	6	4	3

Top-right block:
8	6	3	4	5	2	7	9	1
9	2	5	7	1	8	3	4	6
1	7	4	9	6	3	8	2	5
5	9	7	8	4	1	2	6	3
6	3	2	5	7	9	4	1	8
4	1	8	2	3	6	5	7	9

Central horizontal band:
7	5	8	3	6	4	9	1	2	3	8	5	7	4	6	1	8	5	9	3	2
3	1	4	2	8	9	5	7	6	4	2	1	3	8	9	6	2	4	1	5	7
9	2	6	7	5	1	8	3	4	7	9	6	2	5	1	3	9	7	6	8	4

Central vertical band:
7	8	5	9	3	4	1	6	2
1	4	3	8	6	2	5	9	7
6	2	9	1	5	7	4	3	8

Bottom-left block:
3	2	7	1	6	9	4	5	8	2	1	9
4	6	1	5	8	3	2	9	7	6	4	3
8	9	5	2	7	4	3	6	1	5	7	8
2	1	4	9	5	7	8	3	6			
9	8	6	3	1	2	7	4	5			
7	5	3	6	4	8	9	1	2			
6	7	8	4	9	1	5	2	3			
1	4	2	7	3	5	6	8	9			
5	3	9	8	2	6	1	7	4			

Bottom-right block:
6	7	3	9	2	5	1	8	4
8	1	5	3	6	4	2	7	9
9	2	4	8	7	1	3	6	5
3	6	7	2	5	8	9	4	1
1	9	8	6	4	3	5	2	7
5	4	2	7	1	9	8	3	6
2	8	6	1	9	7	4	5	3
4	3	1	5	8	6	7	9	2
7	5	9	4	3	2	6	1	8

LEFT PUZZLE 25 Reaching 9

Carter's completed grid should look as shown right.

■	1	2	■
■	■	6	5
9	■	3	■
8	7	4	■

RIGHT PUZZLE 1 On the Wild Side

The answer is 3. It's all about changes in relative size—the hexagons get smaller and the triangles bigger, but they stay in the same relative positions. How hard did you find it? The puzzle tests and develops typically right-brain perception of how parts fit together. Check page 9: Award yourself a mark of 3, 4, or 5 if you got it right and found it easy— proceed to L1, or the next available puzzle in the L sequence. If you found it hard, score 0, 1, or 2—this means you need more practice in typically right-brain thinking; move on to R2.

RIGHT PUZZLE 2 I-man Malfunction

The completed grid should appear as shown right. As a portrait painter, Joy is naturally strong in typically right-brain performance and this helps her with the challenge, which tests the ability to complete patterns. She finds I-man an invaluable help in her studio, not only for fetching and carrying, but also for his ability to make small talk and play preprogrammed music to entertain clients sitting for portraits.

ð	¥	Ω	Σ	Ø	∞	π
Σ	∞	ð	¥	Ω	π	Ø
∞	Ω	π	ð	Σ	Ø	¥
π	ð	Ø	Ω	∞	¥	Σ
Ø	Σ	∞	π	¥	ð	Ω
Ω	Ø	¥	∞	π	Σ	ð
¥	π	Σ	Ø	ð	Ω	∞

RIGHT PUZZLE 3 Black Ship Docking

The right choice is 4. With each step (shown below), the black squares both move one spot clockwise, while the white square moves two spots counterclockwise. Of course, Hud Ysseus is the Odysseus character, pursuing a wandering path through space back to his home planet, iTHACA.

RIGHT PUZZLE 4 Naviback

The first ball in your trip is the black spot on white, the fourth ball in the top row. The backward navigation through the ball display is shown right. Conrad's "Redd Sails in the Sunset" school is popular because its proprietor is a gifted communicator, adept at devising training games that deliver improvements in key skills.

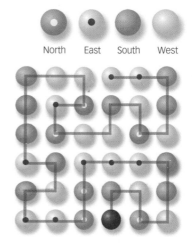

North   East   South   West

RIGHT PUZZLE 5 A@A

The corrrect option is 2, shown right. With each progression, the @ takes the color of the previous little square, the little square takes the color of the previous circle, the circle takes the color of the previous background, and the background takes the color of the previous @.

RIGHT PUZZLE 6 Break-in at Lily-Rose's

The four pieces are A, D, E, and F, as shown right. For more on the mental benefits of looking outward and helping others, check out the website of the Stanford University Center for Compassion and Altruism Research (see page 95). Research has shown that people who act compassionately not only feel better, but also are healthier and live longer. It seems we thrive by helping others rather than seeking to satisfy ourselves.

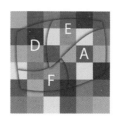

RIGHT PUZZLE 7 Manhattan Mix-up

There is no missing dollar. The cab has $25, the girls have $1 each, and the driver has $2. The confusion arises when you add the girls' $27 to the driver's $2. The $2 should be subtracted from the $27 to make the $25 fare.

RIGHT PUZZLE 8 Unify

B and C fit together. In working on the 2D version of Marcus's block puzzle, you're developing your capacity to visualize 3D objects and to see how things fit together, typically a right-brain strength. It's one with many everyday applications, from building flatpack furniture to getting to grips with how to fit items in a confined space.

RIGHT PUZZLE 9
Blue Period

The ways in (A to B, in black) and out (B to A, in gray) are shown right. The Blue Period heist goes like clockwork. But the boys don't try to sell the painting. They return it to the gallery and win a contract to design and

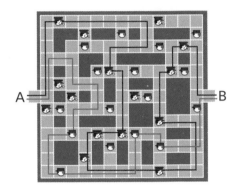

install a new hi-tech security system there.

RIGHT PUZZLE 10 Art's Ark

Art's completed 2x2 grid is shown right. The production focuses not only on pairs (2x2) but also groups of seven (the colors of the rainbow sent by God after the Flood). Art combines design with an interest in recreational math and his staging of the Noah musical is praised for its unusual mathematical angle.

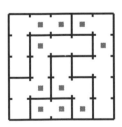

RIGHT PUZZLE 11   Five Hands Five

Polly's opponent is holding these five
cards. Did you ace this challenge?
Did you struggle a little or was it easy

going? Remember to keep an eye on how easy or hard you find the brain
games as you plot your progress through the book.

RIGHT PUZZLE 12   A Philosophical Handyman

Sam's a smart one and knows straightaway what to do: Take a drink
from the machine labeled *tea*. If it's coffee, label that machine *coffee* and
relabel the old coffee machine *soup* and the soup machine *tea*. The old
coffee machine can't contain tea because that would leave the soup
machine with the correct label, and we know that none of the machines
is dispensing the correct drink. Similarly, if the machine labeled *tea*
dispenses soup, then label the soup machine *coffee* and the coffee
machine *tea*. Brain games like this and Right Puzzle 7 are a good
challenge and make an excellent warm-up if you have to address
a difficult problem at work or college.

RIGHT PUZZLE 13 "Happy Happy"

Move from top left to
bottom right: The path
from Happy to Happier is
as shown (right). The new
room turns out to be a big
hit at the Newcycle club.
Harlow finds punters enjoy
using the room on many
different theme nights,
including rave, techno,

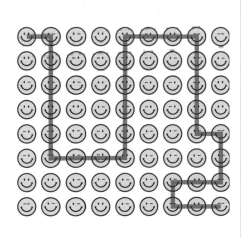

disco, ska and rockin' blues, and even reggae—when the moves across
the grid in the Happy Happy room are made at a gentler pace.

RIGHT PUZZLE 14
Sunetrart

The complete Sunetrart poster design with shaded squares should look as shown right. Develop your typically right-brain capacity to see how patterns and elements connect with puzzles like this.

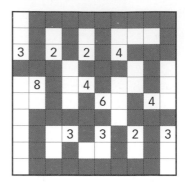

RIGHT PUZZLE 15
Sir Christopher's Chess Position

The pieces should be in the positions shown, right.

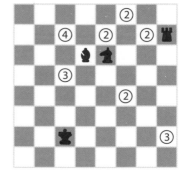

RIGHT PUZZLE 16   Crop Circle Abstract

C is the odd one out. A and B are the same, as are D and E. The puzzle tests and develops the typically right-brain ability to recognize likenesses and differences, and to understand how things fit together.

RIGHT PUZZLE 17
Honeycomb at "Sphere"

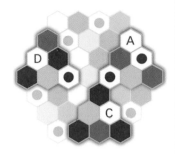

B is not in the grid, but A, C, and D are, as shown right. Niels Bohr's insight (see page 51) would appeal to Sammy McLintock—for it suggests that thinking is like jazz. Just as the solution can be extrapolated from the materials of a problem, so all the variations and experiments of a jazz piece are drawn out from the initial theme that is stated at its beginning.

RIGHT PUZZLE 18   Maurice Moves On

Four of Clubs. The value of each card is the difference between the values of the two cards beneath it, plus three. From top to bottom, along the rows, the suit sequence is repeated in the order: Clubs, Diamonds, Spades, Hearts. Amit has set to work with the information that 4C forms part of the map coordinates of Maurice's hiding place. The Napoleon quote on page 53 (see thinking tip) is also a maxim favoured by Andrew Jackson, seventh president of the United States (1829–37).

RIGHT PUZZLE 19   Temple Wall

E, as shown (right). There are twenty-four ways of arranging the four squares. This is the missing one. Because of the preponderance of designs showing combinations of mathematical planes, the lost society behind the temple becomes known as "the Planes people."

RIGHT PUZZLE 20   King for the Day

Put six cakes on each side of the scale. Remove the cakes on the lighter side, then, from the heavier side, put three cakes each on either side of the scale. Remove the cakes from the lighter side. Finally, from the three cakes on the heavier side, remove one, and, from the other two, put one on either side of the scale. If neither of the two on the scale is heavier, the King Cake is the third of these three (that is, the remaining cake you had removed); otherwise, choose the cake on the heavier side. On the TV reality show, the winner of the King for the Day actually gets to be king for a weekend in the sealed "King Palace" while TV cameras look on and viewers eagerly drink in the shenanigans. The winner of this challenge was housewife Rupinder, who naturally became Queen for the Weekend.

RIGHT PUZZLE 21   Party Like It's 2099

The seven hexagons should be aligned as shown right. As we have seen, when you judge how elements combine within a larger design this is a typically right-brain process.

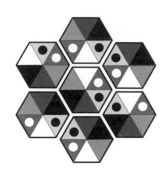

RIGHT PUZZLE 22   They Walked Free

A = 2/dark gray, B = 8/light gray, C = plain black, as shown. Each row and column contains three black squares, two dark gray squares, and two light gray squares, plus numbers that total 20. The escape was planned for February 8th, at midnight (the plain black square being code for the middle of the night). Heinrich Baum was not able to crack the code. Were you? In the movie, the prisoners escaped despite a number of escalating difficulties, and made it to the coast, where they were picked up by British operative Roger Hockney in a battered sailing vessel.

RIGHT PUZZLE 23 Chez Alexandre

The completed grid is shown right.
Alexandre has empty electronic grids
hung on the wall and wired up to tablet
computers on the tabletops in the café.
As visitors enjoy their drinks and meals,
they fill in the grids on the computers
and the shaded designs appear on the
wall-mounted grids. In this way the wall
designs change every day. Alexandre's

grids are full-color, so this adds vibrancy to his establishment.

RIGHT PUZZLE 24 Interlock

This is how to solve Käthe's puzzle.

Across: Adding rows B and C, two Clubs, two Hearts, one Diamond, and
one Spade total 130. There is one of each suit in row A, totaling 90. Thus,
subtracting a Spade, a Diamond, a Club, and a Heart from rows B and C
would leave one Club and one Heart. Together the Club and Heart total
130 (rows B and C) minus 90 (row A), thus one Club + one Heart = 40. So
one Spade + one Diamond = 50 (row A). Thus a Spade = 30 (row D) and
a Diamond = 20. A Club = 15 (row B) and a Heart = 25 (row C). Thus:

• Heart = 25, Club = 15, Diamond = 20, Spade = 30

Down: Comparing columns B and C, a Diamond is worth three more than
a Spade. Comparing columns B and D, a Diamond is worth five less than a
Heart. So (column A) Spade + Diamond + Heart + Spade = (Diamond – 3) +
Diamond + (Diamond + 5) + (Diamond – 3) = 59, so four Diamonds = 60,
thus one Diamond = 15. A Club = 7 (column B). A Spade = 12 and a Heart
= 20 (above). Thus:

• Heart = 20, Club = 7, Diamond = 15, Spade = 12

RIGHT PUZZLE 25 Polly's Aria

The solution is shown right. At the
premiere, Polly's aria brings down
the house.

THINKING CHALLENGE 1 "The Trouble I've Seen"

How you set about memorizing the travelers' names and details reveals a good deal about your brain balance. A typically left-brain approach is to focus on facts and linguistic elements—to note, perhaps, that Marco and Nisha's names begin with consecutive letters, that Rebecca and Carter's ages add up to 50. A right-brain approach is to focus more on people's appearance—for example, the fact that Carter and Rebecca are linked not only by being a couple but also in both having brown eyes, that Sir Charles and Andrew (another couple) are the only two with facial hair.

The two men who approach you to ask about conversion rates are Marco and Jonty. For their currency conversion, Wodehouse and Williams is the best bet if you have a large sum to convert. SmartCash works out at €9,750. Harrington offers €10,500 minus a fee of €525 = €9,975. Wodehouse and Williams is €11,250 minus a €1,125 fee = €10,125. If you feel confident with this, you're exhibiting typically left-brain numerical ability. If the task panics you, then your natural strengths are more in the right brain and you'd benefit from working on the left puzzles in the book.

How do you approach memorizing the room bookings? Do you visualize their position in the building—from Rebecca and Carter in the basement to Jonty on the rooftop? It's simple enough to link the room names to their positions—it makes sense, sure enough, for the penthouse to be treetop and the sky pavilion to be on the roof … This is a predominantly right-brain approach. Alternatively, you might focus on names and numbers.

What about the room decorations? An ability to judge colors, shapes, and pleasing combinations is typically right-brain. If you're not confident in this area, you're seen as principally left brain and you'd benefit from working through the right-brain puzzles. How do you manage in remembering appropriate refreshments? Do you recall that Marco must be spared milk products since he's lactose intolerant and that neither Jonty (recovering alcoholic) nor Rebecca (teetotal) must be offered alcoholic beverages?

And how do you respond to the problem with the bags? You have twenty-one bags and space for only eighteen! A typically left-brain response would be to order up another van, but a person with right-brain strengths can often see how things fit together. If you have this capacity, you might work out a way to fit them all in … If they really can't, perhaps you'd think intuitively around the problem—again taking a typically right-brain approach—and use your space in the taxi to have the bags transported to the hotel? You can walk, since it's only a mile away.

For each of the five elements of the challenge:
- If you strongly favor right-brain processing score 3.
- If you mildly favor right-brain processing score 2.
- If you strongly favor left-brain processing score 1.
- If you mildly favor left-brain processing score 0.

Left-Brain/Right-Brain Questionnaire

Questions 1, 2, 4, 7, 9: If you agree, you tend more toward right-brain processing. Score 2 for each question you ticked.
Questions 3, 5, 6, 8, 10: If you agree, you tend more toward left-brain processing. Score 1 for each question you ticked.

Combine your score for Thinking Challenge 1 with your score on the questionnaire to get your **Starting Score**. Our aim is to balance your thinking, so if your score indicates you are strong in right-brain thinking, start with a left-brain puzzle. Conversely, if your score suggests you excel at left-brain tasks, begin with a right-brain puzzle.

- **If you scored 21 or more,** start with Left Puzzle 1.
- **If you scored 13–20,** start with either Left or Right Puzzle 1.
- **If you scored 12 or less,** start with Right Puzzle 1.

THINKING CHALLENGE 2 "Summertime"

Can you rise to the challenge of making a speech with little or no notice? If so, you're strong in left-brain performance—either by nature or because you've built up your left-brain strength by working through this book.

The calculation required to work out the monies due is also typically left-brain work; however, scientists report that the concentration you need to hold your attention on a matter like this despite distractions depends upon right-brain operation. The total due is $2,685. The 7.5 percent tip is around $200 (exactly: $201.38). You give him $205.

As we've seen, an ability to combine shapes and colors is typically right-brain. In the challenge you text through your choice of color scheme and décor and it makes a well-judged setting for Hugo's dishes. Then you have to commit the directions to memory. A more right-brain person will focus on landmarks: Louis Armstrong statue, cycle taxi rank, etc.; a left-brain approach is to focus on the street names: Waterside, right along May Way, etc. If possible when committing things to memory, try to link facts with interesting related information … sing "I Did It My Way" to fix May Way, say.

And how to soften the blow of the missing limos? You may have noticed the cycle taxi rank, and you could phone ahead to book some cycle taxis for your guests—even to ask them to meet you at the dock. This would appeal to Carter. Then you make sure the taxis stop at the Louis Armstrong statue as Marco is a jazz trumpeter. As a fan yourself, you know that August 4 was Armstrong's date of birth and that today (August 4, 2016) is in fact the 115th anniversary of his birth. This would add weight to your argument, as would the fact that it is a beautiful day for a cycle ride.

An ability to achieve an overview, to use your intuition and creativity to come up with a new way of presenting what has to happen, engages the right brain; but your adroit use of persuasive language relies on your left brain. As you have worked through the book, you have no doubt identified which modes of thinking you are more at ease with; you have tackled puzzles and brain games designed to support and raise your performance in less natural areas of cognition—helping to balance your thinking.

How Did You Do?

Now, why not count up how many of each number you scored to get an idea of your overall performance. Here's an idea of what it means:

- Mostly 5s—you're a genius! Your thinking is balanced but it never hurts to get more practice.
- Mostly 4s—pretty impressive. Maybe you found some of the puzzles a bit difficult, but you got there in the end.
- Mostly 3s—well done, you persevered. Even if you struggled with some puzzles, you kept going. You're on the way to balancing your thinking.
- Mostly 2s—good effort. You didn't give up, even if some of the puzzles got the better of you. Keep trying and you'll find you begin to improve.
- Mostly 1s—practice makes perfect. The more you stretch your brain, the more you'll fine-tune your thinking and the greater the benefits.
- Mostly 0s—don't be disheartened. Perhaps most of the puzzles had you stumped, but keep stretching your brain and you will notice a difference.

Further Reading & Resources

Books

At Left Brain, Turn Right: An Uncommon Path to Shutting Up Your Inner Critic, Giving Fear the Finger & Having an Amazing Life! by Anthony Meindl, Meta Creative 2012

The Bhagavad Gita According to Gandhi, ed. by John Strohmeier, North Atlantic Books 2009

Brain-Balance Workout by Charles Phillips, Connections Book Publishing 2013

Left Brain, Right Brain: Perspectives from Cognitive Neuroscience by Sally P. Springer and Georg Deutsch, Worth Publishers 1997

The Master and His Emissary: The Divided Brain and the Making of the Western World by Iain McGilchrist, Yale University Press 2012

Rewire: Digital Cosmopolitans in the Age of Connection by Ethan Zuckerman, W.W. Norton 2013

Smarter: The New Science of Building Brain Power by Dan Hurley, Viking 2014

Surfaces and Essences: Analogy as the Fuel and Fire of Thinking by Douglas Hofstadter and Emmanuel Sander, Basic Books 2013

You are the Music by Victoria Williamson, Icon Books 2014

Websites

Altruism: The Stanford University Center for Compassion and Altruism Research (CCARE): http://ccare.stanford.edu/blog/

Meditation guidance: www.easwaran.org

Peace and nonviolence: www.mettacenter.org

TED Talk: Ethan Zuckerman "Listening to global voices": www.ted.com/talks/ethan_zuckerman

The Author

Charles Phillips is the author of more than 35 books, including *Stay Smart*, *Brain-Balance Workout*, the Brain Builder series, and *Business Brain Trainer*, as well as eight volumes in the best-selling How to Think series. Charles has also investigated Indian theories of intelligence and consciousness in *Ancient Civilizations* (2005), probed the brain's dreaming mechanism in *My Dream Journal* (2003), and examined how we perceive and respond to color in his *Color for Life* (2004).

EDDISON•SADD EDITIONS
Concept Nick Eddison
Managing Editor Tessa Monina
Designer Brazzle Atkins
Production Sarah Rooney

BIBELOT LTD
Editor Ali Moore
Puzzle-checker Sarah Barlow

PUZZLE PROVIDERS
Guy Campbell; Clarity Media;
Laurence May (Vexus Puzzle Design); Puzzle Press